THIS IS MY CLASSROOM

École K.L.O. Middle School Eco Leaders

Amber	Jasmine
Ben F	Jordan
Ben H	Katelyn
Ben S	Maddie
Brian	Madelyn
Carrie	Madison
Cassie	Mikera
Celia	Mitchell
Dana	Natasha
Daylath	Pru
Esme	Samantha
Hayley	Tyson
Hiro	Will
Ian	Wesley

SPECIAL THANKS:
The École K.L.O. Middle School Teachers, Staff, Parents, and Alumni, The K.L.O. Green Committee, The Central Okanagan Naturalist Club, Michelle Hamilton, Shane Driscoll, Karla Lockwood, Emily MacMillen, Denise Kenney, Nancy Holmes, UBC, and The City of Kelowna.

THIS IS MY CLASSROOM

PREFACE

My name is Shimshon Obadia, I am an artist and researcher leading 'Daylighting the Classroom,' a project in partnership with The University of British Columbia's SSHRC funded Eco Art Incubator research initiative, running out of École K.L.O. Middle School in Kelowna, B.C.. This project's mandate is to use eco art to re-envision education and the role of the natural world in school curricula. For the past year, I have been using eco-art to connect middle school students with their more-than-human community. This project is also designed to bring attention to these students' now seven-year struggle to restore the often flooded concrete-covered wetland habitat that once ran through their school grounds. Initiated by students' discovery of blue-listed Western Painted Turtle eggs in their long jump sand pits, this school's community, with the guidance of science and environment teacher Michelle Hamilton, began to restore the species' disappearing habitat. Originally challenged to raise $100,000 by their school board for this habitat's restoration, multiple "generations" of students remarkably raised $86,000. Unfortunately, in an updated quote, these students recently discovered their project will now cost half a million dollars. Although dismayed and disappointed, through work on this issue, the students and teachers involved ended up creating a process of discovery- how the natural world is an educational resource gold mine. Through eco art implementation in their education, these students have shown an aptitude for learning far beyond what is regularly observed of middle school students in a traditional classroom setting. This project focuses on the completion of this endeavour, cultivating these students' inspiring passion for their environment, defining the role of eco art in the classroom and in school curricula, and helping students negotiate the disappointments and obstacles of bureaucratic intransigence and even, some might say, of dismissal of children's right to learn from and steward the natural world.

It has been an absolute pleasure working with these students and getting them reconnected with their natural world through creativity. The more I work with them, the more I am inspired and filled with hope for the future of our world; I know its caretakers are moving in the right direction when I see the action these students are taking. In all this, I feel as if I have only been the catalyst giving them the tools they ask for to be able to make their ideals and dreams reality. This is not the slactivist generation usually associated with preteens; when given direct creative exposure and experiences with nature, these "slactivists" can change the world. In this book, 'This is my Classroom,' the students at École K.L.O. Middle School have put together, in a variety of mediums, a compilation of creative reflections; these are focused on who and what they see as their more-than-human educators which they have found in their natural environment. As well as showing the rewards of the 'Daylighting the Classroom' project, this book is directly contributing towards this community's long term habitat re-naturalization project for the Western Painted Turtles on the École K.L.O. Middle School campus. All funds from the sale of these books go directly towards the creation of an outdoor learning environment which will be mutually beneficial for its human students as well as its more-than-human students like those new, wide eyed Western Painted Turtles that hatch here every year with a whole world of opportunity to discover.

TO LEARN MORE ABOUT THE **DAYLIGHTING THE CLASSROOM PROJECT** OR TO DISCOVER MORE ECO ART INITIATIVES HAPPENING IN THE OKANAGAN VALLEY

VISIT

www.EcoArtIncubator.com

&

www.ShimshonObadia.com

All different colours.
Being taught how to survive
Soaring through the sky

Haiku

Turtle eggs hatching
Concrete in Creek, annoying
People trying hard

A. To stop this madness
A. That is just creating sadness
B. We believe it is not fair
B. To cut a species life in pairs

A. Spliting a creek in two
B. By a fat concrete bridge
B. But us middle school kids
A. Demand something new

A. We want something changed
A. Not what we have irranged
B. We need to have this pass
B. For outside is our true class

Orange, green, brown, yellow
Gently blowing in the wind
Grow roots to survive

A feeling,
Reading a book under an apple tree,
When the weather is right,
And the breeze brings the scent of apples,
Peaceful and blissful.
I never said an emotion,
But you thought of one right?

A place,
Snow has recently covered the ground,
No cars have pushed it off the roads,
No winds have blown snow off the trees,
No driveways have been shovelled.
I never said where, but you pictured it, right?

A Story,
The one you pictured reading under the apple tree,
It has transported you to different places,
You and the characters have laughed,
You have cried, you are best friends.
I never gave a title, but you thought of one, right?

A person,
Their face, immediately recognisable,
Too familiar for words,
Their expression,
The way they talk
I never gave a name, but you thought about them, right?

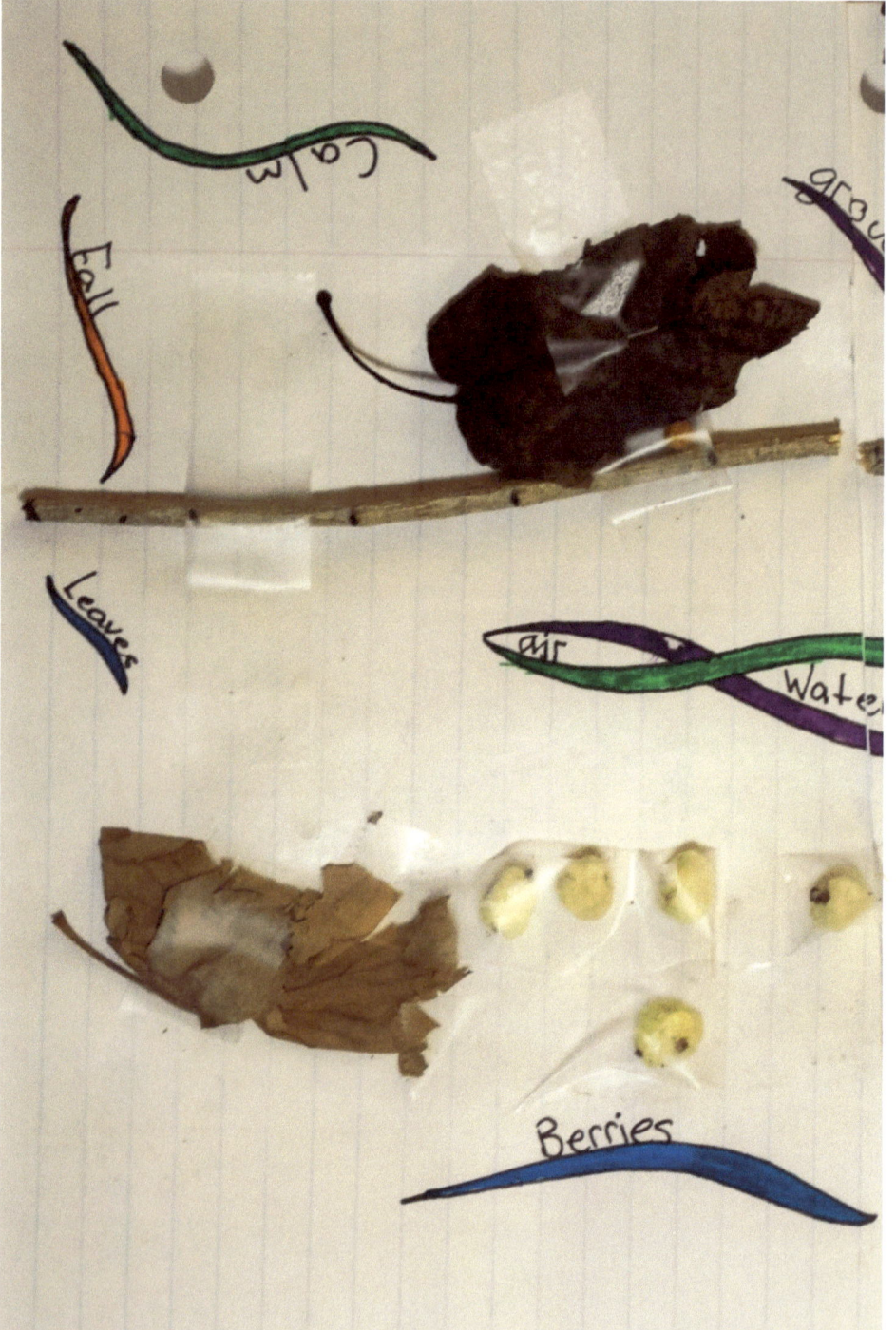

Once covered by green

Now has a lot of concrete

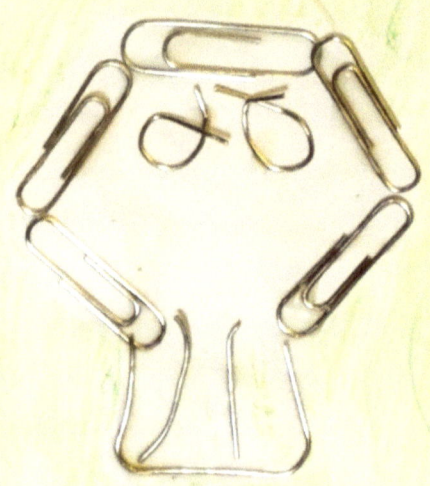

only you can help

The dancing flowers sing,
  as the sun rises in the spring.
My heart feels warm and like its glowing,
  The white caps are rolling and flowing.
  In the distance the pine trees stand,
  They will live forever in our classroom land.

Beautiful designs are spread on wings.
The splats and puddles of colours bring,
cheerfulness in the summer soil,
and they shine like gleaming foil.
Butterflies are what we love,
  and always wanting more of.

Spines start to stiffen,
ice grows and glistens.
The earth slowly freezes,
and brings in chilly breezes.
We look around,
everything's alone,
nothing here but ice and snow.

But soon the land awakens again,
and the rainbows shine,
through the freshly born rain.

By Madison Brown

Will Tanner

The valley, a huge expanse waiting to envelope the shadows of the mountains. Towering white peaks reaching out to the sky. I try, I fail,... I Improve. This is the place were we build memories, the place where we test abilities, have adventures. Learning is haveing these expiriences. From trail and error, crashes and recoveries, I am separated from the mountian only by the two wheels and the handle bars beneath me.

Stale air, white light burning my eyes eyes. a cold plastic chair that I sit on. No windows, making my skin go pale. This square blank class room cooping me up, leading to depresion. This is the stale, lablike environment in that I learn.

Seeing an endangered species,
a once in a lifetime experience.
Watching a bird observe the forest,
wanting to get closer but keeping distance.
Enjoying the bird's beautiful colours,
enjoying the sound of its unique call. ♪

The smell of the forest,
fresh and pure,
the warm sun is heating the land.
The animals are insecure,
they are questioning why I am here.

The bird flies away now,
Searching for food,
It flies quickly but with great control.

Wondering where it will find food,
hoping it will remain safe.

I know that what I've seen is special,
Most people rarely see what I have seen.

After lowering my binoculars,
I start towards the trail,
anticipating what great things lie ahead.

Mountains

Towering over everything

The skyscrapers of forests

Snow blanketing the giant peaks

Each one calm and tranquil

From small hills to mighty mountains,

Standing still and sturdy

Foggy mist blocking the strong rock

This is my classroom

The Fallen Leaves are Stories from Old Trees

Little Leaf

Lay down

Let your green
turn into brown

You'll grow back again

Carbon dioxide + trees = air

Animal - forest = no home

Forest ÷ people = destruction

Rain + plant + sunlight = grow

Male + Female = Baby

Welcome to Our Class

We are a special class
Were not like any other
When we choose to learn
We do it out in nature

Helping the community

Fixing up our creek

Building gardens

And composting

Fundraising, nature walking and planting.
These are a few things that we do for nature.

Hiro Kobayashi

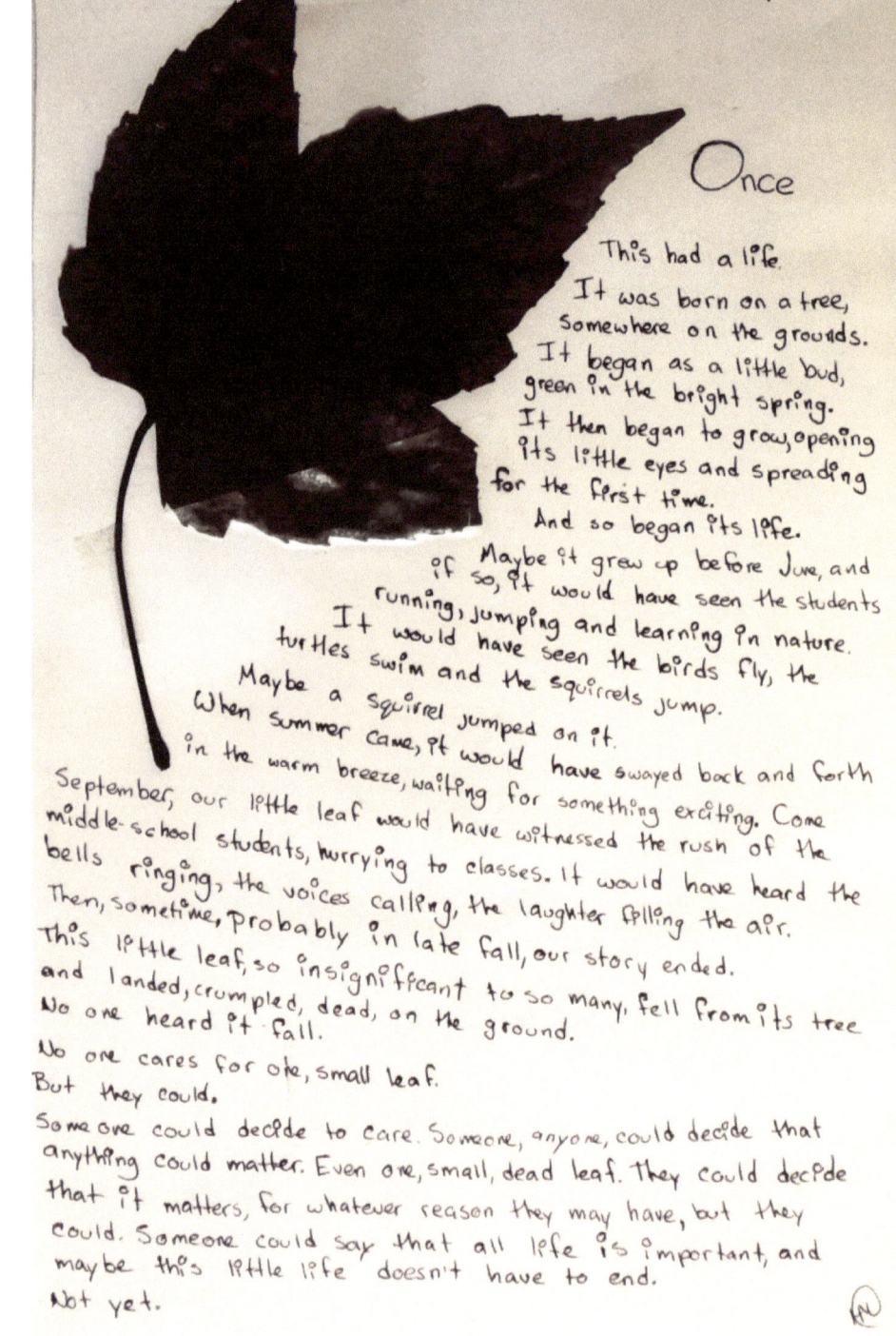

Once

This had a life.
It was born on a tree, somewhere on the grounds. It began as a little bud, green in the bright spring. It then began to grow, opening its little eyes and spreading for the first time.
And so began its life.

Maybe it grew up before June, and if so, it would have seen the students running, jumping and learning in nature. It would have seen the birds fly, the turtles swim and the squirrels jump. Maybe a squirrel jumped on it. When summer came, it would have swayed back and forth in the warm breeze, waiting for something exciting. Come September, our little leaf would have witnessed the rush of the middle-school students, hurrying to classes. It would have heard the bells ringing, the voices calling, the laughter filling the air. Then, sometime, probably in late fall, our story ended. This little leaf, so insignificant to so many, fell from its tree and landed, crumpled, dead, on the ground.
No one heard it fall.
No one cares for one, small leaf.
But they could.
Someone could decide to care. Someone, anyone, could decide that anything could matter. Even one, small, dead leaf. They could decide that it matters, for whatever reason they may have, but they could. Someone could say that all life is important, and maybe this little life doesn't have to end.
Not yet.

THIS IS OUR
CLASSROOM IN NATURE

Hiro Kobayashi

Turtals are hachang in the long jump pits and hibernate under the snow.

The duck has a brown or green head. A yellow or orange bill and brown legs. Some have handle bar moastashes made out of snow.

BenF.

Wild rye^2 ÷ Winter = Snow^2

Snow^2 = Snowballs × −12°C

−12°C = frozen creek

−12°C ÷ 2 = frozen puddles

−12°C ÷ 1 = frozen fingers

−12°C

I try
To take advantage of the space outside
That you've given me
Instead of a room full of binders and desks
But i'll have to wait and see
See if this time will never end
If I can ever go inside again
I see
That I could spend a million years out here
a never ending classroom
that radiates reality
But i'll have to wait and see
See if this time will ever end
If I can ever go inside again

THIS IS MY CLASSROOM

AFTERWARD

Today's middle school students, like the Eco Leaders at École K.L.O. Middle School, have a near infinite amount of information at their fingertips. Through an educational mandate called '21st Century Education' which the British Columbia ministry of education has been incorporating into its curricula more and more each year, students are not only able to connect to this overwhelmingly vast array of information but are learning how better to access it instead of just learning how to memorize it. As far as I am concerned, this is a move in the right direction but what often gets missed in curricular documents about 21st Century Education is that the internet is not the only information database available to students.

'This is My Classroom' is a small press publication project I created with the Eco Leadership students at École K.L.O. Middle School. We used this project as a vehicle to build a creative and embodied knowledge of the natural more-than-human world around them to use as a database instead of, what Richard Louv calls, "the know-it-all state of mind" in his book 'Last Child in the Woods,' for students to be more balanced in their understanding of their knowledge.

Louv's philosophy is that "children need nature for the healthy development of their senses, and, therefore, for learning and creativity. This need is revealed in two ways: by an examination of what happens to the senses of the young when they lose connection with nature, and by witnessing the sensory magic that occurs when young people—even those beyond childhood—are exposed to even the smallest direct experience of a natural setting." This is a kind of knowledge that must be engaged through the human body, making use of all of its sensory interphases, it simply cannot be fully understood in binary code alone.

To start this project, the students and I went on a series of walks through the school grounds they themselves had worked extensively to re-naturalize. In our note books, we collected dead leaves, branches, and other decomposing matter, as well as took notes on how we responded to our environment and how it responded to us. We then went through a crash course on the small press and self publication process, learning from examples made by local artists and self-publishers. The material created out of the embodied data we had collected and documented ranged from paintings, to poems, to decomposing material on the page, to math equations, and stories. Each one of these contributions shares the unique perspective of each student's direct and embodied experience with their more-than-human counterparts.

In the process of creating this book, it did take a while before students started doing more than what specific method I was showing as an example each day for their submissions, and then taking ownership eventually over their creative input to the book. But once they realized they had that ability and artistic license, their work began to blossom. Through this process, I learned that less direct guidance (being less didactic) can be better for creativity and the acquisition of knowledge; as people need to discover this particular kind of knowledge, not simply be told what it is.

www.ingramcontent.com/pod-product-compliance
Lightning Source LLC
Chambersburg PA
CBHW041404090426
42743CB00006B/149